MISSISSIPPI
ALPHABET

WRITTEN AND ILLUSTRATED BY
LAURIE PARKER

QUAIL RIDGE PRESS • Brandon, Mississippi

Dedication

For Joey and Elizabeth Gray

Walter Anderson Alligator courtesy of the family of Walter Anderson
Photograph of B.B. King courtesy of the Delta Blues Museum
All other photographs courtesy of the Mississippi Department of
Economic and Community Development and the Mississippi
Department of Archives and History

Printed in South Korea by Tara TPS

9 8 7 6 5 4

Library of Congress Cataloging-in-Publication Data

Parker, Laurie, 1963 –
  Mississippi Alphabet / written and illustrated by Laurie Parker.
  p. cm.
  Summary: An alphabet book about things in or relating to
Mississippi, from azaleas and armadillos to Yazoo and the
great Jackson zoo.
  ISBN 0-937552-92-5
  1. Mississippi– Juvenile literature. 2. English language–Alphabet–
Juvenile literature. (1. Mississippi. 2. Alphabet.)
I. Title.
F341.3.P37 1998   98-23274
976.2(E)–dc21   CIP
                                                            AC

QUAIL RIDGE PRESS
P. O. Box 123 • Brandon, MS 39043 • 1-800-343-1583
info@quailridge.com • www.quailridge.com

MISSISSIPPI

has fun things to know and to see.

Let's hear about some of them

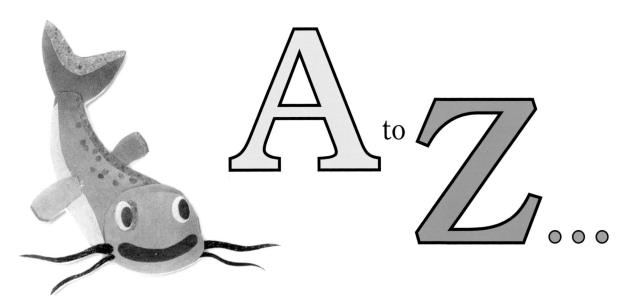

A to Z...

A is the letter with which we will start.
And what is A for?

Walter ANDERSON's ART!

A's for AZALEAS that bloom in the spring
And it's for ARMADILLO—a strange-looking thing!
Old Southern homes that are lovely to view
Are called ANTEBELLUM. That starts with A, too!

ABERDEEN   AMORY   ANGUILLA

ARTESIA

ALGOMA

Aa

ARCOLA

ARKABUTLA

AVALON

ACKERMAN   ASHLAND   ALLIGATOR

BAY ST. LOUIS BYHALIA BELZONI BILOXI

BATESVILLE

BAY SPRINGS

BROOKHAVEN

BOONEVILLE

Bb

BOGUE CHITTO BRANDON BALDWYN BOBO

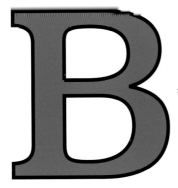

B's for BILOXI, a town on our coast
And the big International BALLET that we host.

B is for B.B.
You bet!
B.B. King!

And B's for the
BLUES that
he really could sing.

B is for BALLGAMES on bright afternoons,
BARBECUE, BUTTERBEANS, hot-air BALLOONS,
And don't forget BULLY, the dog fans adore...

Yes, in our Mississippi, that's what B is for!

C

is for **COTTON**
grown here on our land

And the **CAPITOL** building
where state laws are planned.

C is for **CATFISH**, farm-raised in a pond
And our own Jerry **CLOWER** of whom we're so fond.

There's the **CANTON** Flea Market where folks come to browse,

And **CHURCHES**

and **CHICKEN**

and **CORNBREAD**

and **COWS!**

Cc

COLUMBUS CORINTH CANTON CLEVELAND

COLDWATER

CRYSTAL SPRINGS

CLINTON CHARLESTON CARTHAGE

COLUMBIA CLARKSDALE COLLINS CALHOUN CITY

DECATUR   DE KALB   DARLING   DREW

DE SOTO

DUCK HILL

DODDSVILLE

DUNCAN

Dd

D'IBERVILLE   DERMA   D'LO   DURANT

D is for DAIRIES that operate here
And D is for DOGWOODS and D is for DEER.

D is for DELTA

as flat as can be

And two early explorers whose names start with D:

They're Hernando DE SOTO and D'IBERVILLE
And if you've never studied about them, you will!

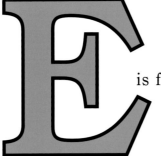

E is for ELVIS, the rock 'n' roll king.
What else is E for?

Oh, there's many a thing!

Our writer, Miss Welty's first name is

EUDORA

And we have E towns here and there—

Like EUPORA.

F is for **FAULKNER**, another famed writer

And **FORESTS** that make our state greener and brighter.

F is for **FARMS** on which our state depends,

The **FAIRGROUNDS** and **FESTIVALS**,

FAMILIES and **FRIENDS**.

G

is for GRISHAM. His books surely sell.

And G's for the
GOVERNOR'S MANSION
as well.

G's also for GOSPEL, but we are not through,
'Cause we've got G city names here—quite a few!

There's GREENVILLE, there's GREENWOOD,
and farther away
Along the GULF COAST,
there's GULFPORT and GAUTIER!

H stands for a word for which our state's known:
HOSPITALITY!
Something we always have shown.

H is for HATTIESBURG and for HOLLY SPRINGS

And HUMMINGBIRDS

HOMETOWNS

And more happy things

Like yummy HUSHPUPPIES that we like to eat
And wild HONEYSUCKLE, so fragrant and sweet.

INDIANOLA   ITTA BENA IUKA

Ii

ISOLA   INVERNESS   INGOMAR

Mississippi has lots of **I** words we can claim.

I's for the **INDIANS** who gave us our name.

I is for **INDUSTRY**. That helps us thrive
And I is for **INTERSTATE I-55!**

I is for **ISLANDS** like Ship, Horn, and Cat
And it's for homemade **ICE CREAM**—it's fun to make that!

JACKSON's a place that begins with a  **J**

And it's the state capital, too, by the way.

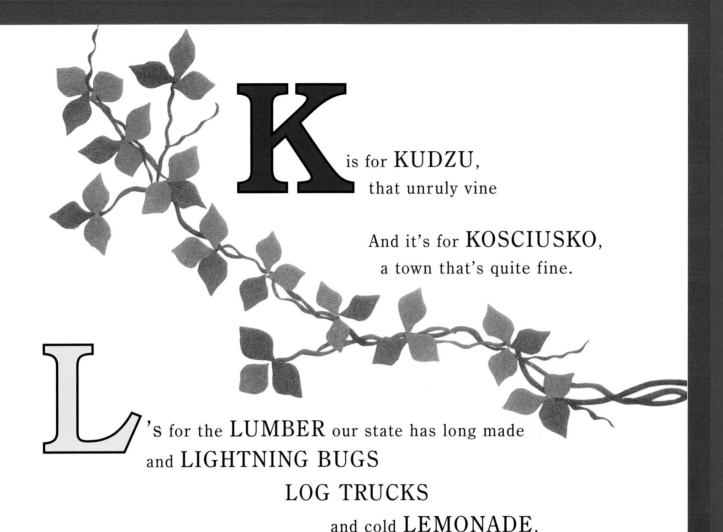

K is for KUDZU,
that unruly vine

And it's for KOSCIUSKO,
a town that's quite fine.

L's for the LUMBER our state has long made
and LIGHTNING BUGS
LOG TRUCKS
and cold LEMONADE.

L is for LEONTYNE—Leontyne Price
And our LAKES where the boating and fishing are nice.

LAUREL LEAKESVILLE LUCEDALE LENA

LONG BEACH LIBERTY LORMAN

LAUDERDALE LEXINGTON

LULA LELAND LUMBERTON LOUISVILLE

Ll

MAGEE MERIDIAN MCCOMB MAGNOLIA MIZE

MOORHEAD MERIGOLD MONTICELLO

MENDENHALL MOSS POINT MARKS

Mm

MADISON MOUND BAYOU MORTON MACON

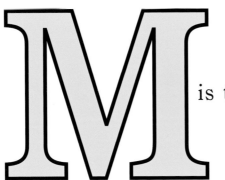

M is the letter that stands for our state

And for many more things
we have here that are great.

M is for MOCKINGBIRD—that's our state bird.
Our flower, MAGNOLIA's another M word.

And M is for MUD CAKE, MIMOSA, MOON PIE,
And MERIDIAN. That's a neat city nearby.

 is for **NATCHEZ**,
the Trace
and the town
And it's for **NANIH WAIYA**, an Indian mound.

A county that's known for its fair starts with N—
NESHOBA! Their county fair's big. Have you been?

O's for
OLD
CAPITOL...
but that's not all.

O is for OAK TREES,
majestic and tall.

O is for OXFORD, a town with a square
And O is for OLE MISS, the school that is there.

A star who has roots in our state starts with O—
She's OPRAH, of course! She was born here, you know!

P

P's for PECANS and for PINES—common trees
And POSSUMS
　　　　and PEACHES

and PURPLE-HULL PEAS!

P is for PILGRIMAGE.　P's for PLANTATION
And for our state PARKS where we have recreation.

P is for PORCHES where people can sit
And it's for the PEARL RIVER...have you heard of it?

PASCAGOULA PICAYUNE PETAL PONTOTOC

PICKENS PURVIS PHILADELPHIA

PRENTISS PLANTERSVILLE PEARL

Pp

POPLARVILLE PORT GIBSON PELAHATCHIE

Q is for one of our birds here—
the QUAIL

And QUITMAN,
the town and the county as well.

R's for the RIVER
that shares our state's name

And RAILROADS that brought Jimmie RODGERS his fame.

Even more Mississippi things start with an R:
ROCKING CHAIRS, RED CLAY, and yes...RESERVOIR!

S

is for **SHRIMP** that are caught off our coast

And the **SHIPBUILDING** there
of which we can boast.

S is for **SOYBEANS**

and

SORGHUM

and

SQUIRRELS

And **SWINGS**, made for swinging, for young boys and girls.

Tt

TIPPO

TISHOMINGO

TULA

TOCCOPOLA

TOOMSUBA

T is for iced TEA and TURNIP GREENS...yum!
And T is for TUPELO...they hope you'll come!

There's the TOMBIGBEE River that runs through our state
And counties like TUNICA, TIPPAH, and TATE.

U

UNIVERSITY—that word begins with a U.
USM's one. Can you name other ones, too?

V is for VICKSBURG, a Civil War site,
And long, fancy porches...VERANDAS! That's right!

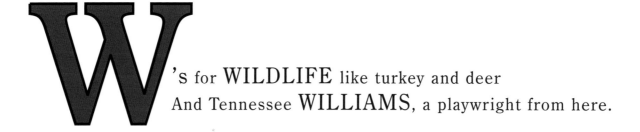

W's for **WILDLIFE** like turkey and deer
And Tennessee **WILLIAMS**, a playwright from here.

There's also **WISTERIA**, wonderful smellin',
Old **WAVERLY** Golf Course, and mmm...**WATERMELON**!

All these good things make our state so inviting.
In fact, Mississippi is

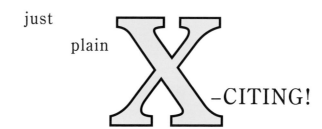

just
plain **X**-CITING!

WAVELAND   WINONA   WEST POINT   WEBB

WEIR

WALNUT

WOODVILLE

WAYNESBORO   WATER VALLEY   WIGGINS

WALNUT GROVE

WESSON

Ww

Now, **Y** is not such a hard letter at all.
It's for two words we say down here: YONDER and Y'ALL.

And it's for YALOBUSHA. Gosh, that's tough to spell.
It's the name of a county and river as well.
Another Y word we have here is YAZOO—
The city, the county, and kind of clay, too.

And now we've got just one more letter to do.

It's **Z**

And it stands for
our great Jackson

ZOO!